the
EVERYDAY
EVANGELIST

the EVERYDAY EVANGELIST

Developed by Duncan McIntosh

Editor: Laura Alden
Consultant: Jan DeWitt

Judson Press®
Valley Forge

THE EVERYDAY EVANGELIST

Copyright © 1984
Judson Press, Valley Forge, PA 19482-0851

Third Printing, 1986

Unless otherwise indicated, Scripture quotations are
from the Good News Bible, the Bible in Today's
English Version, Copyright © American Bible Society,
1976. Used by permission.

Other quotations of the Bible are from the Revised
Standard Version of the Bible copyrighted 1946, 1952 ©
1971, 1973 by the Division of Christian Education of the
National Council of the Churches of Christ in the
U.S.A., and used by permission.

Library of Congress Cataloging in Publication Data

McIntosh, Duncan.
  The everyday evangelist.

  1. Evangelistic work. 2. Witness bearing
(Christianity) I. Title.
BV3790.M48 1984   248'.5   83-22169
ISBN 0-8170-1042-4

The name JUDSON PRESS is registered as a trademark
in the U.S. Patent Office.
Printed in the U.S.A. ⊕

FOREWORD

"Meet them where they are," said Phillips Brooks, "and lead them to the foot of the cross."

This book attempts to help people do just that. For too long, we as evangelicals have tried to win people to Jesus Christ by beginning where *we* are. *The Everyday Evangelist* says that we need to listen before we tell. To begin an evangelistic conversation by talking about personal sin when that individual is asking "Why does God let bad things happen to good people?" is patently ridiculous. We need to get to know the deep concerns of those to whom we witness and direct our message to meet them at the point of their needs.

This book is unique. It is given a strong, theological base by Dr. Duncan McIntosh of the evangelism staff of the American Baptist Churches in the U.S.A.: "The Good News is the story of thousands of years of God's active loving—beginning with creation, continuing in the divine guidance of ancient Israel, reaching a high point in the life, death and resurrection of Jesus Christ and culminating in the establishment of the kingdom."

Written for laypersons, the book can be used as a study for congregations interested in training for personal evangelism. Study guides are provided for each chapter. Encouragement is given for learning one's own "faith story." Prayer is shown to be absolutely necessary. And the power of the Holy Spirit is recognized as crucial for the energizing of the whole enterprise.

Biblical *models* are studied: Jesus and the Samaritan woman, Paul and the people of Athens, Peter and the Jews, Jesus and the rich, young ruler, Philip and the Ethiopian official and others. All are researched for cultural identity, emotional needs and spiritual beliefs in order to understand the approach to be made to such persons.

We are grateful to Jan DeWitt who provided valuable consultation for educational process. Special thanks go to Laura Alden, our evangelism staff editor, who put the book into its present form and to Joanne Powers, Grace Bickley and Judy McLaughlin who typed the manuscript.

The Everyday Evangelist. Carefully chosen, the title says that evangelism is done by laypersons who, between Sundays, best live out the drama of salvation through Jesus Christ. I commend its reading and careful study.

Emmett V. Johnson, Director of Evangelism
American Baptist Churches in the U.S.A.

September 1983

INTRODUCTION

"When I was younger," said the preacher, "I had lots of enthusiasm for sharing my faith. I talked about Jesus everywhere, especially at the grocery store where I worked. I invited every employee there (and as many customers as I could) to follow Jesus.

"Of course I didn't think much about the fact that because of all my 'witnessing' I sometimes slighted my work. After all, I was busy doing the work of the Lord. The other employees even called me 'Preacher.' That was a sign that my witness was having some effect, I thought.

"And then one day I found out exactly what that effect was. Though the employees called me Preacher to my face, behind my back, because of how I worked, they called me the 'creeping Jesus.'

"The next summer I had a job on a construction crew. Determined not to repeat my mistake, I worked harder than anyone else. I figured the others would notice and wonder why.

"They noticed me all right. But not for the right reasons. Finally, at the end of the summer, one of the guys came up to me and said, 'So, you're going to be a preacher.'

" 'Yes, I am,' I replied eagerly.

" 'I don't think you'll be too good at it,' he said. 'You don't talk about religion enough!' "

There is a definite dilemma associated with evangelism. It's evident in the example above. Stated simply, the dilemma is: how?

In recent years the word "evangelism" has been used to describe quite a range of activities and styles of communicating. It has been used to refer to evangelists who preach God's Good News with honesty and integrity. It has been used to describe the sincere sharing of personal faith which Christians have practiced through the centuries. But "evangelism" has also become a label for the proclamation of formulas which may have no significance to those who hear them. It has been used to describe the activity of those who request cash gifts rather than faith commitments. And it has been the name applied to a "hellfire and brimstone" style of preaching.

Such excesses can undercut the very meaning of evangelism. For the word "evangelism" is derived from "evangel," which means *Good* News! To do evangelism is to communicate this Good News. It is to offer a dynamic alternative to those who seek spiritual and personal identity, to those who seek relationship with God and with those around them, to those who seek peace—both spiritual and temporal, to those who seek meaning in life and in death. Evangelism makes faith an option for the seeker.

The knowledge that we once lived outside of faith should encourage, if not obligate, us to be evangelists—to tell what we know of God's Good News. "If we ourselves have been captivated by Christ," says George Peck,"at some point we must inevitably be moved to share him with another."[1] If we really believe in a God who rules, a Savior who lives and a Spirit who works through us to change the world, we cannot be silent!

The cock crows. And we are convicted of our mission: "[It is the will of] God our savior...that every human being should find salvation and come to know the truth. For there is one God, and also one mediator between God and humanity, Christ Jesus, himself human, who sacrificed himself to win freedom for all humankind, so providing at the fitting time, proof of the divine purpose; of this I was appointed herald and apostle...to instruct the nations in the true faith" (I Timothy 2:3b-7, paraphrased).[2]

Some of us may be called to share our faith to a particular group of people in a certain culture. But most of us are called to share faith with those around us—the people we know. We are called to relate what we know of God to individuals. This "personalized" evangelism can take into account the varying needs and backgrounds of people—both of the evangelist and of the person who hears the gospel. To be sure, the plot of the story we tell is the same. But because the characters in it are always different, the story of God's love needs to be told in different ways, ways relevant to those characters.

Francois Mauriac said about the characters in his novels, "The human being as I conceive him in the novel is a being caught up in the drama of salvation, even if he doesn't know it."

This book has been written to help Christians who desire to bring that drama of salvation to the consciousness of those around them. It has been.written to instruct the "everyday evangelist."

CHAPTER ONE

She was sitting on a park bench at lunchtime, eating a peanut butter sandwich, feeding the pigeons and reading a devotional book.

The man next to her asked, "What are you reading?"

She showed him the title.

"Oh." The man was disappointed. "A religious book . . . . I used to be religious."

"Used to be?"

"Yeah. But that bowing and scraping got to me. Didn't mean anything . . . ."

"Nothing?"

"Not really . . . . Oops! One o'clock meeting. Better go."

The man walked away. But he almost wished he had stayed. Something had stirred inside when he remembered his religious experience. He turned around and waved at her, hoping she would come back to that bench.

The pigeons hoped so, too.

Part of knowing how to share the Good News is knowing what it means—what makes it good. Many people have had the empty religious experience of the man in the example above. They have not experienced the "Good" News. They may have heard only "Repent!" and not "Be saved!" Or they've been asked, "Are you saved?" and never understood why they needed saving. Others have practiced religious forms but have never known God. Because of these experiences, many people, our friends and family members among them, have concluded that all religion is inadequate and not worth the effort it demands.

What is the Good News we have to share with people such as these? It is *great* news! It truly is "the greatest story ever told."

John told it this way:

"For God *loved* the world so much,
   the greatest love

"that he *gave* his only Son,
   the greatest gift

"so that *everyone* who believes in him
   the greatest offer

"may not die but have *eternal* life"
   the greatest promise

(John 3:16).

The Good News is the story of thousands of years of God's active loving—beginning with creation, continuing in the divine guidance of ancient Israel, reaching a high point in the life, death and resurrection of Jesus Christ and culminating in the establishment of the kingdom.

The Good News is the story of a Creator's love. It is a story which began with the expression—and rejection—of God's love. It is God's story and our story.

Love Expressed / Love Rejected

"Let there be...!" said God.

And there was light by day, light by night. There were oceans, rivers, lakes and streams. Trees and dry land. Fish, fowl and furry animals. And finally, man and woman.

"And God saw that it was good" (Genesis 1:31). All of it. God put man and woman in charge of the creation—to care for it, to keep it good. God gave them knowledge of their Creator. And God, their sovereign and their shaper, loved them and sought their companionship (Genesis 1, 2).

But the man and the woman denied their maker. They rejected God's authority and ran from God's intimacy. They separated themselves from the source of their lives and took their future and the destiny of creation into their own hands.

This is what the Bible calls sin—the willful turning away from God. Sin separates creature from Creator, inverting the natural order. There must be a returning to God, a reconciliation of people with their Creator for creature and creation to survive.

And there was.

Love Restated / Love Accepted

Through prophets and priests, kings and teachers, God sought to restore the broken relationship. Then, in the grandest statement of love ever conceived, God sent Jesus to represent divine love on earth (Galatians 4:4-5). Jesus, as the Son of God, proclaimed the possibility of restoration for both body and spirit. The condition of this restoration, said Jesus, was response—a turning from sin, a turning to God. For those who chose to believe and act on this Good News, there was reconciliation and reunion with God (Romans 5:1).

Jesus made this reconciliation possible for all people. For God allowed him to be put to death, to suffer separation from God for us, thereby giving us all a chance to turn back to the source of life and receive *new* life that could not be quenched (II Corinthians 5).

Love Empowered / Love Obeyed

So we are saved because Jesus died and lived again—and because we believe he did. We are saved from eternal physical death as well as spiritual death because Jesus overcame death in the resurrection.

As believers, we are once again God's children and therefore, brothers and sisters to each other. That relationship requires us to grow together and to be a blessing to all families on earth (Genesis 12:1-3).

The Spirit of God, present in all who believe (John 14:25-27), empowers us to live in this relationship and to translate the story of God's love into the language of personal experience. It is then that God's story becomes our story. And when that happens, we know it to be true.

Witness, then, is the translation of God's story into personal experience. This is not to say that there is no objective truth or spiritual reality beyond experience. "The Story of Love" illustrates that. See page 14. But to many people, especially to those with whom we share the Gospel, faith appears most credible in terms of "how it happened" to someone they know. Witnesses testify to what they have experienced. We have experienced reconciliation and reunion with God. Therefore, that is our witness.

Paul describes our role this way:

Here we are, then, speaking for Christ, as though God himself were making his appeal through us. We plead on Christ's behalf: let God change you from enemies into his friends! (II Corinthians 5:20).

Other translations say we are "ambassadors for Christ." As such, we are part of the diplomatic corps of the kingdom. Our mission is to ask people to change from being enemies of God to being friends—to

THE STORY OF LOVE

GOD'S INITIATIVE

Love Expressed
God is Creator. God is love. God expressed love in creation.

Love is experienced through relationships. God offers us relationship.

Love Restated
Rejection does not stop God's love. God's love was restated in a completely new way in Jesus. Through the life, death and resurrection of Jesus, it is now possible for all to love God and others in restored relationships.

Love Empowered
Through the Holy Spirit we are included in the fellowship of believers. We are enabled to produce the "fruits of the Spirit" in our lives. We are equipped with gifts for ministry.

HUMAN RESPONSE

Love Rejected
We resist accountability to God. We resist the love of our Creator.

We try to control our own lives and destinies, we reject relationship with God. This rejection is called sin.

Love Accepted
We may choose to give our lives over to God's control.

When we acknowledge Jesus as Lord and Savior, our past rejection is forgiven and we are set free to become who God created us to be.

Love Obeyed
We live as believers by praying and studying the Bible, by participating in a local church, by sharing God's love with others and by faithful service in the world.

bring about reconciliation. For that is what has happened in our lives.

Sin separates us from God; reconciliation joins us to God. Those who are reconciled to God and to each other make up the church.

Sound good? A world reconciled. A world at peace.

It sounds heavenly. And it is. Reconciliation is the goal toward which we strive, an impossible goal made possible only by the Spirit of God at work in us and in the world.

So we have confidence, knowing that the Spirit of God is our partner in bringing about this reconciliation. For the Spirit of God is experienced beyond all limits of time, space and culture (John 1:32). God's work was done before the time of Jesus by the Spirit of God. From the Gospels we know that the Spirit was on Jesus himself (John 1:32). Jesus told his disciples that after he was gone, the Spirit would enable them to continue the work he had begun (John 14:16-29).

The Spirit works in the world to bring people to an awareness of God (John 16:7-11). Then the Spirit works to bring the seeker and the evangelist together so that the seeker may find new life in Christ (Acts 8:29).

If we do not believe the Spirit is at work, our motivation for mission will be weakened. But if we do believe, we can confidently join in the task, knowing we are following One who has prepared the way and knowing that when we witness, we are simply giving voice and life to the Spirit's presence and power at work in those with whom we share.

The pigeons waited patiently. So did the man who had come back to the park bench, wondering if the woman would come back, too.

And she did, bag lunch and book in hand.

CHAPTER TWO

"Hi. Still reading your book?" he asked her.

"Yes. This is about the only time I have to read," she said.

"And so you use it to read about religion."

She smiled and unwrapped her sandwich. "It's good for me."

"I took a religion class in school," he said. "It was interesting, but didn't change my mind much."

"Where'd you go to school?"

"The University. Business major, like everyone else. Wanted to be a musician. But you can't like to eat if you're a musician."

She laughed. "Tell me about it," she said. "That's why I teach instead of perform."

"You're a musician?"

"Well, I teach at the conservatory."

"Close enough," he said, and tossed a crust to the pigeons.

Knowing why and what we are to share, we must consider how we are to share it! How do we go about retranslating God's Story of Love into words that make sense to individuals with varying needs and different backgrounds?

One of the first things we can do is relax. Faith is meant to be shared, not shoved at someone. It is our responsibility, yes, to tell the story, but we are not responsible to convict or convert people. God, the Holy Spirit, does that. The Spirit gives us both the words to say and the opportunity to say them. Our sensitivity to what to say and when to speak can be heightened by prayer and by allowing ourselves to be led to those who are ready to hear the story of God's love.

This means we are not compulsive or guilt-ridden ("I should say something") about sharing our faith. It means we listen prayerfully for the threads of God's story woven into the lives of others by the Holy Spirit. Then we can help individuals recognize their place in that story.

In order to enable others to identify God in their lives, we must be certain we can identify God in our lives. We must be able to tell our version of God's story. Our experience with faith, told to another, can make God's story credible to someone who views faith as abstract. Our witness can make it concrete.

Every Christian has had personal experiences of God's saving and guiding grace. These are often forgotten when we become absorbed in everyday needs and routines. It is a good exercise for both our faith and our memories to recall how we realized and now realize our part in God's story.

Review now how God's story has been acted out in your experience. The way you experience faith has much to do with your background, interests, abilities and needs. Fill in, think about or discuss with another the following autobiography. Reflect on the fact that each of your answers may be a thread which could connect you to someone with similar ideas and images who may need to hear the gospel.

1. Describe your family:
   The kind of housing you live in:
   Your job:
   What you do well:
   How you spend your money:
   Your favorite pastime:
   Your favorite TV show(s):
   Your favorite kind of music:
   Your favorite daydream:

2. The greatest need in your life has been:

3. How do you picture God (as a judge, parent, lover, comforter, distant ruler)?

4. What place does Jesus have in your life?

5. In light of who you are culturally, emotionally and spiritually, what approach to faith would have turned you away from God?

6. What approach caught your interest?

Some Christians can recall a single life-changing moment when they first believed. Others of us were nurtured into faith, "surrendering," as Sam Shoemaker said, "as much of ourselves as we understood to as much of Christ as we understood" along the way. Regardless of the type of conversion we experienced, there have been additional occasions when we have been made particularly aware of God's presence.

Think now of those times. You may want to list them on the chart called "Steps of Faith." Indicate your age when these incidents occurred. Go back as far into your childhood as possible. See pages 20 and 21.

Now that you've thought about how God has worked in the past, it is necessary to become aware of the current leading of Jesus Christ in your life if your faith is growing and vital. The easiest way to do this is to build the habit of at least weekly focusing on some specific experience in which the presence and power of God were especially real to you.

Some Christians keep a daily journal as part of a devotional time. You may wish to try this, taking time to reflect on your experiences, asking, "What can I learn through this?" Keeping a journal can also enrich your prayer life as you see specific items for thanksgiving, confession or intercession. It is fascinating to look back on your journal after a period of time and see how God has helped you through times of stress and difficulty as well as in times of joy and new opportunity. By keeping a record of God's work in your life, your story remains current.

Another way to update your faith story is to agree with one or more friends to share on a regular basis. Each of you should agree to make a point of sharing the current dynamic of your faith—what God is doing in your life right now—and discussing the meaning it has for you (see Romans 1:11-12). The agreement should include sharing low experiences when it seems that God is absent or silent, as well as the high experiences when God is doing great and obvious works in your life. This same type of sharing could also be done with a small support group.

This sharing should include a time of prayer. Pray for the members, the other evangelists, in your group. And pray for those with whom you will share the Gospel. Praying for specific individuals will help you identify with whom you should share and make you sensitive to the needs of those persons.

Because of who you are, you will be led to represent God to certain people at certain times. While God wants all people to turn back to their Creator through Christ, because of differences in personality and differences in your experiences there are some people with whom you can more easily relate than others. Perhaps you will relate better to persons with whom you have something in common. Often, problems can help you relate to others with similar problems (II Corinthians 1:4). More often than not, we don't lack for people with whom we can relate well, people who

STEPS OF FAITH
(example)

Experience	Age
• "accepted Jesus into my heart"	7
• "rededicated" my life to Christ	12
• baptism and pastor's class	14
• involvement in youth mission trip	16
• move away from home	18
• small group summer Bible Study	21
• birth of first child	24
• dedication of first child	24
• marital problems and counseling	33
• divorce	35
• illness of mom/her recovery	37
• friendship with another Christian	37
• involvement in support group	37

MY FAITH STORY

(example)

Grandpa — 0-12

Summer Camp — 13-17

18-25

My friend Paul, who wouldn't let me be satisfied with casual belief — 26-37

38-45

Dad's death (& new life!) — 46-65

65+

Age

STEPS OF FAITH

Experience   **Age**

•

•

•

•

•

•

•

•

•

•

If you have trouble identifying specific experiences, refer to the chart entitled "My Faith Story." Place a check at the points you remember experiencing God's presence and guidance in a special way. Or write above each age grouping one or two words that identify people or events which influenced you.

MY FAITH STORY

Age
   0-12   13-17   18-25   26-37   38-46   45-65   65+

also need to hear of God's love for them. They are the people of our everyday lives—neighbors, co-workers, fellow students, carpoolers, landlords and landladies, family members, casual acquaintances.

Concentrate now on the people you know for whom Christ is not the object of faith. Spend time in prayer asking God on which three people you should concentrate. Then write their names on a card and prop the card in a place where you will see it often and be reminded to pray for them.

We have referred to the need to be relaxed, to be familiar with our own version of God's story, to pray for our own efforts and the efforts of others, to concentrate on specific individuals. Now we need to listen.

Before God acted redemptively, God listened. When God heard the cries of the oppressed people in Egypt, Moses was sent to take them out of their bondage. When the rebellious young nation of Israel fell under the control of other nations and cried for deliverance, God sent the judges and later the prophets. Finally, in response to centuries of questions, God took on the form of a servant to set men and women free from their doubts and to proclaim the answer of acceptance. God listened to the needs of people and then took action.

Jesus was a storyteller. But he also listened to the stories of those he met. He listened not only with his ears but with his heart. He knew what was in the hearts of others (John 2:25) and spoke in words and ways which responded to their needs.

Story listening is the ability to hear the truth that others tell in their stories. Unfortunately many of us are better storytellers than we are story listeners! It is not unusual to have someone else's story trigger a chapter in our own experience. When our story comes to mind, it is tempting to share it before the other person has finished. When we do this, we switch the focus from the other person to ourselves. A mother, in describing something that her children experienced, said, "We could see what was happening but we did not know why." Many of us as listeners would have to say, "We could hear their words, but we didn't take time to understand their meaning."

If we care about others, we must train ourselves to hear what they are really saying. As you listen, you will begin to discover how to introduce God's story to individuals in the way he or she can hear it best.

Some people have great difficulty speaking about themselves. Often they will make personal statements by talking about the problems of others. People who feel weak and inferior may try to appear strong and speak with deliberation and firmness. A frightened person may appear to be very aggressive and controlled.

As a caring evangelist then, you must listen to the three people for whom you have decided to pray and on whom you will be focusing your attention. If you listen carefully, you will hear their questions and begin to understand their needs.

Recently a mother and her college son were driving by a church. On its roof was a large sign which said, "Jesus saves." When asked his reaction to the sign, he said, "None." When she asked what kind of sign would catch his eye, he said, "Free doughnuts."

After a good laugh, she said, "You do believe that sign, don't you?" He said, "Yes, but it's answering a question I'm not asking." When asked what question he was asking, he said, "What should I do with my life? What career should I pursue? Whom should I marry? How can I be strong in my faith?" The mother asked what sign would speak to him. The boy thought for a moment and then said, "I don't know but I sure wish someone would design one."

If we listen to others carefully, we will be more likely to hear the questions being asked. Then we can refer to those questions in talking about faith. We will never use a memorized script because although the plot is the same, the characters will always be different.

Lunch was over. He was sorry.

They had talked about music. And about other things. He wondered if he had talked too much.

No. She had actually seemed interested, even when he had put down her faith. She wasn't like the other religious people he knew. She had listened and hadn't tried to argue. He felt better than he had in months.

"See you tomorrow," he said.

CHAPTER THREE

They looked forward to the park bench lunches, those pigeons. Five days a week the two friends met, so the pigeons thought, to feed them.

"Maybe I could give you a few violin lessons," she said one day.

"Oh, I'm too old for that," he responded, hoping she'd disagree.

"Bad excuse," she said. "Right after work. Okay?"

In our efforts to learn how to tell God's Story of Love to others in words they will hear and understand, we can look to the Bible for models. In studying encounters between people, we'll analyze how evangelism was done then and look for principles which can be used in personal evangelism today.

The Model: Jesus and the Samaritan woman (John 4:1-42).

First, read the text and note what you can about the society in which the Samaritan woman lived. If you have access to a commentary or a Bible dictionary you can read about the barriers that existed between the Jews and Samaritans. Compare your notes with those which follow: The trouble between them had been going on for over 400 years. When the Assyrians invaded Israel's Northern Kingdom, they captured many Jews, carrying them back to Assyria. People from Babylon and other places moved into the Northern Kingdom, mingling with the Jews left behind. Then, in the days of Ezra and Nehemiah, the exiles returned and began rebuilding the temple. The local Samaritans came to offer help but were spurned by the Jews of the Southern Kingdom because the Samaritans had intermarried with foreigners. The Samaritans had lost their "racial purity," even though they still considered themselves Jews. Through the years other incidents had added fuel to the quarrel.

In addition to this racism, there was sexism. Women in ancient Israel were second-class citizens. Men did not speak to them in public. And the Samaritan woman was of an outcast class of women. She had had many husbands.

It is significant then that Jesus even spoke to the Samaritan woman for in doing so, he was bridging a gap not only of race and sex, but of social class.

Now, using this background, imagine that you are the Samaritan woman, but that you are living in the twentieth century. What kind of person are you? Put yourself in her place; see things through her eyes. (This exercise is fun to do in a group study situation.)

Describe your family:
The kind of housing you live in:
Your job:
What you do well:
How you spend your money:
Your favorite pastime:
Your favorite TV show(s):
Your favorite kind of music:
Your favorite daydream:

You have just become acquainted with a modern-day Samaritan woman. That is, you have perceived her personality in terms of culture. This understanding will aid your analysis of the evangelistic style Jesus used in sharing with her.

Another way to know a person is to learn about the "inner person," about his or her thoughts and feelings. In order to accomplish this part of our analysis, we need to take a look at emotional needs.

The choices and decisions the Samaritan woman made and that we make in our lives are influenced by certain basic needs. The needs may be manifested in different ways, but we all strive for SECURITY, AFFECTION, ESTEEM and GROWTH.

All of these needs are present to some extent in our daily lives but some are more important to us at certain times than at others. For example, people with SECURITY needs are concerned with having adequate food, clothing, shelter and money for themselves and their families. Personal safety from danger is also a major concern. People with security needs are likely to shy away from taking risks and will be hesitant to try new things. This reluctance carries over into other areas as well; they will usually be slow to trust someone else and slow to accept what they consider to be new ideas. They need a friend they can count on, a friend who can guide them into the knowledge of a God they can count on.

People with AFFECTION needs desire to be included in a group; they need to feel they belong; they need to be loved. They will even try to force friendships, acting out of fear and loneliness. They need to be invited into a caring group of people and learn of a God who cares for them and who has even prepared a place for them.

People with ESTEEM needs want to be seen as significant. They need to be recognized for specific reasons, to be treated by others with respect and to have their opinions considered. They need to be encouraged to become involved in service and to see service as a response to the Servant.

People with GROWTH needs desire to be stretched, to experience new things. They like challenges and long to expand their horizons, improve themselves or gain deeper understanding of their lives. They want to be all they were meant to be and live on the "growing edge." They need to be challenged with opportunities through which they will learn. They need friendship from the "movers and thinkers" of the faith, people who will show them that faith is life's greatest challenge.

We all have these needs and they must be met continually for us to be fulfilled. (For a moment, look back at your autobiography and see which of these four categories applies to you right now.)

Our needs influence our thoughts about faith. They can also prepare people for faith. Think about this principle in relation to the case of the Samaritan woman. You have made her a contemporary woman in terms of culture. Now do the same with her in terms of emotional needs. How might she respond to the question:

What are the greatest needs in your life right now?

You may have identified her needs as affection, esteem and/or growth. She may have been searching for love in her relationships with men. But the consequences of that search (her several marriages) may have lowered her respect for herself. She probably needed to see her potential as a person and experience a higher degree of self-esteem. She was a seeker; she wanted to know more about God, to grow.

In addition to having a cultural identity and emotional needs, there is no doubt that the Samaritan woman had, as all humans do, a spiritual dimension to her personality. Through the ages, people have attempted to understand themselves and others by reaching out to a supreme deity and formulating belief systems. Becoming aware of the way a person sees God helps determine how to share God's story with him or her. Again, as an exercise, put yourself in the role of the Samaritan woman and answer the following question:

How do you picture God?

The woman believed in God as a distant sovereign. She was waiting to find out more about God. She believed a Messiah would come.

Now summarize what you know about this woman. Answer the following question:

In light of who you are culturally, emotionally and spiritually, what approach to faith would turn you away from God?

An approach which would have turned her away would be one which judged or threatened her. She had already been judged by those around her. She could also have been turned away by an approach which dismissed her belief.

What approach would catch your interest?

An approach which would catch her interest would be a personal and caring encounter, one which would see beyond her reputation, to the potentially "good person" she could be. This encounter would be even more effective if the evangelist validated her own belief in God and offered her further instruction.

You have probably recognized that this is a format similar to the one you used in your autobiography. Everyone, whether living in Bible times or today, can be viewed culturally, emotionally and spiritually. With practice, God's Story of Love can be adapted to every person's background.

As you look at the passage, it is obvious that Jesus was aware of the Samaritan woman's background. It is also obvious that his approach was tailored to her—and that his approach was effective.

Think back to the analysis you did of the Samaritan

woman. In light of what you know of her, note how Jesus approached her.

The location was familiar to the woman. Jesus initiated the conversation, making the social situation more comfortable. He treated her with respect and was willing to listen to her. He recognized her potential, but did not pressure her.

He began with something they had in common. Then he presented God's story in words she could understand, validating her belief and explaining God's offer of new life to her. He helped her see herself in terms of her life situation. (Not until a person has a sense of conviction about his or her need for help can we tell him or her the Good News of God's story). Jesus did not share the details with his disciples.

The result of this encounter was that the Samaritan woman saw herself—and her community—in a new way, in relationship to Christ.

From our analysis of this encounter, how can we summarize Jesus' treatment of the Samaritan woman (given the facts that he knew her background and her needs)?

He treated her as a friend would have.

That conclusion should lead you, as an evangelist, to do the same—both with the three people you have identified and with others—as you seek to communicate God's story. Based on the example of Jesus, here are four steps to be used in building friendships that could lead to the sharing of faith.

1. Make friendships a priority. It is easy to say that we value friendships and then spend little time with our friends. Friendships can all too easily be blocked by "busyness." Real friendships require time. If we are to build an open and trusting relationship with another, the friendship must take priority over other activities.

Jesus had space in his daily living for other people. Yet he never neglected his own need for quiet time, especially his need for prayer time. If other people were to receive from him, Jesus had to be prepared. Just because people were a priority did not mean that they took first place in his life. God occupied first place in Jesus' life. That is why "retreats" were important to him.

Determine now when you will talk to a friend to set a time for getting together. Pray about it and then act. Before you meet your friend, check your calendar to see when you might be free another time. Don't leave your meeting to chance. Plan your next meeting together.

2. Accept others. This seems hard for us to do. We struggle over how to accept people without necessarily condoning what they may do or how they may act. Yet each of us does something similar to that when accepting a gift we don't really like. We say that the thought counts more than the object. When we thank the giver, we mean it. We accept him or her as a friend but we don't attach ourselves to the gift.

That is how Jesus related to people. He dealt with what kept them from becoming all that God intended them to be. He saw them in the way that God saw them—in terms of their potential.

If we are to be a friend to someone, we must see him or her as a person of worth. We need to accept people as God accepts them. We should not regard them merely as souls who need "saving" but as unique persons whom God can set free and empower for the work of the kingdom. Our acceptance becomes a living example of God's acceptance. They will come to understand and experience the acceptance of God as we live it out with them.

3. Listen actively. It requires conscious effort to move beyond words in order to "hear" the nonverbal clues given by a person in tone of voice, facial expressions and the choice and order of words. But that effort must be made if we are really to hear what is being said.

Active listening will help us determine our friends' background and needs. Every day we hear people tell of their daily experiences—often in the form of stories. These stories are not fiction. They are the daily experiences of people which reveal their spiritural quests. These stories might be compared with an antique chest that one comes upon at an auction. Because the chest is so intricately carved it is easy to become absorbed in examining only the outside of it. Yet, if we were to lift the lid, we might find something far more wondrous inside than what was outside.

Every "story" we hear hides a truth like a treasure hidden inside a chest. Most people are unaware of all they are sharing as they narrate their everyday stories. As we listen to them, we can begin to discover how to introduce God to that person at the point of his or her interest and need.

You don't have to be a psychologist. Your friend's words and ways will tell you a lot about him or her. (Refer to the blank biography at the end of this chapter if you wish to record clues that will help you in determining needs.) People who desire material things may need security or esteem. People who are always doing things to please others may need to feel esteem or affection. Those who always seem to be doing new things may need security or growth. By practicing active listening and keen observation, you will find yourself more able to distinguish one need from another.

Listening will also help you discover the religious convictions of your friends. In speech and behavior, people give clues to their beliefs. These clues must be matched up to the part of God's story that will be Good News for the seeker. Listen actively first. Then ask yourself how you can relate God's love to that person in the most natural and direct way.

By listening, you will be able to determine whether your friends need your companionship, your actions or your words. Listening will also help you determine which words are the most important and meaningful at that moment. Here you must be especially aware of the input of the Holy Spirit. As the evangelist, you are a channel through which God relates to your friends. As Jesus did, so you must listen actively both to God and to those with whom you share.

One who listens carefully is one who learns much about others. This obligates you to keep confidence with your friends. It is imperative that you refrain from relating what you know to anyone—not even as a concern for prayer. You can ask another Christian friend to pray for someone without revealing identity or sensitive information. If you break confidence, your credibility as a friend and as a witness will be lowered. If your friend can't trust you, Christ's representative, how can he or she trust Christ?

4. Share. Listening draws you silently into the lives of others. Sharing draws you vocally into their lives. Sharing is the act of two who receive and give. Following are some guidelines to help you in sharing.

Be open to learning new things about others and about yourself. This is important if you are relating to someone who is committed to and follows another religious persuasion. If you want that person to learn something of your faith, shouldn't you be open to learning something about his or hers? You may discover things to affirm in the other person's faith as well as find openings to speak of the uniqueness of Jesus Christ.

This openness may lead you to try new activities. Imagine how you would feel if someone asked you to introduce him or her to your hobby or favorite pastime. If your friend bowls and you never have, why not give it a try together? Or try a new kind of music or a new kind of food.

Sharing is also doing things you both enjoy. Don't neglect interests you have in common. Do things together. Go places together.

The most important part of sharing is the communication of your faith in Jesus Christ and the introduction of others into the fellowship of the church. Jesus Christ is an important part of your life as a Christian. That should not be hidden from a friend any more than the fact that you enjoy baseball or like a special flavor of ice cream. Jesus Christ can influence your friends' lives much more than can your taste in desserts or your preference in entertainment.

As a Christian friend you have something unique to share. If you believe this, you will go on to introduce your friends to Jesus Christ. Share what Christ means to you. Share what he does for you. Share what he calls you to do. Then share an invitation to believe.

All of this takes time. There is no doubt that true friendships "cost" in terms of time and energy. "My commandment is this," said Jesus, "love one another, just as I love you. The greatest love a person can have for his friends is to give his life for them. And you are my friends if you do what I command you" (John 15:12-14). To be a conscientious friend may mean it will be necessary for you to give up part of your life—your time and energy—for someone else.

That is what Jesus did for the Samaritan woman. He gave up his pride in speaking to her. (After all, she was a Samaritan as well as a woman of questionable reputation). He gave up his time and his desire to rest in order to spend time with her. He let her talk. He cared about her.

In his treatment of this woman, Jesus is our model. He was an evangelist to the woman at the well, as we are to the people around us.

"Okay," he said. "But let me do something for you then."

She hesitated. "Do you know any other would-be violinists?" she asked finally. "I really could use a few more students."

"You got 'em," he said.

BIOGRAPHY

CULTURAL IDENTITY

Summarize his/her cultural environment:

Describe his/her family:

The kind of housing he/she lives in:

His/her job:

What he/she does well:

How he/she spends money:

Favorite pastime:

Favorite TV show(s):

Favorite kind of music:

Favorite daydream:

EMOTIONAL NEEDS

What are his/her greatest needs?

SPIRITUAL BELIEFS

How does he/she picture God?

Describe his/her beliefs about Jesus.

APPROACHES

In light of his/her cultural, emotional and spiritual orientation, what approach to faith would turn him or her away from God?

What approach would catch his/her interest?

nsamu wambote
ευαγγελιον
Good News
Buenas Nuevas

CHAPTER FOUR

"There's only one thing that keeps me from totally denying the existence of God," he said one day.

She grinned. "I know."

"You do?"

"Sure," she said. *"I'm convinced that nobody who really listens to Bach can deny the existence of God. Bach will haunt you."*

"You do know," he said.

She laughed at his amazement.

God's story has been told in many languages. Music is one. Art is another. Actions and relationships also tell God's story. But at some point God's story, which may have been presented in any number of ways, needs to be translated into words as a summary and invitation to belief.

The apostle John knew this. He wrote his Gospel so that "you may believe that Jesus is the Messiah, the Son of God, and that through your faith in him you may have life" (John 20:31).

His words are powerful in that they give both purpose and promise. The purpose: that you may believe. The promise: that you may have life.

In other words, John wrote this account of Christ's life and work to do more than give expression to his faith. He wrote his Gospel to urge people to believe in Christ.

We are always engaged in the expression of our faith. But evangelizing is more than giving an impression of Jesus to others. It is inviting others to put their trust in him. Words are our vehicles to do this.

For some of us, this is hard to do. We are not "good with words." We fear "saying it wrong." Yet we must speak. Even an intentional caring act can fail to carry the message that God cares if it is done without words of explanation. It can be viewed simply as thoughtfulness.

Couple this with the fact that most church people have a "theological vocabulary" that is relatively unknown to people outside the church and the margin for misunderstanding widens. David Augsburger capsulizes the dilemma in this example of what can happen "in the translation."

Speaker	*Listener*
Since I got saved.	He became thrifty or religious?
I live a victorious life.	He wins all arguments.
I'm set free from sin.	He's lost all interest in sex?
I've a deep settled peace.	Nothing bothers him anymore.
I never get angry or swear.	He must be lying now.
I don't smoke or drink.	No kicks.
I'm living for Jesus.	What does He have to do with this?[3]

When sharing with a friend, you cannot speak in theological terms thinking that these will communicate God's story. There are, after all, very few "theological" words in the Gospels. The words of Jesus were the words of the marketplace, the field, the court, the seaside, the kitchen. Jesus used everyday words to describe God and God's desire for relationship with people. In parables, Jesus took people from the known to the unknown through the use of illustrations from real life. He led them from the temporal to the eternal.

As an evangelist it is your task to meet people where they are—in the here and now—and lead them to the eternal. To do this you must tell, as Christ did, God's story to each person in his or her language. It is essential then to discover some of the key words in the language of your friends and use these words to tell God's story. To someone interested in physical fitness, you might speak of faith in terms of disciplined habits and activities which grow out of commitment. If someone has been ill, physically or mentally, you could talk about God's gift of "wholeness." For someone burned out you might speak of "renewal." For someone environmentally aware you could speak of how God "recreates." Then, you can naturally ask those persons if they would be willing to trust in a God who relates to their needs and interests, who created them the way they are and whose only Son came to earth to bring about their salvation.

In the two models which follow, we will see how this is done—how Paul and Peter took the languages of their hearers and turned them into the language of faith. Both men used what they knew of the faith of their listeners to point to the true Author of faith.

Model No.1: Paul and the people of Athens (Acts 17:16-34).

Study this passage, looking for details that describe these people. (To supplement your information, you may wish to refer to a Bible dictionary or commentary.)

Now think of yourself as one of these people. Refer to the biography at the end of chapter 3 and think through the questions. Jot down your responses. Then compare your responses to those which follow.

THE PEOPLE OF ATHENS

CULTURAL IDENTITY

The Athenians were intellectuals who enjoyed discussing ideas. They were mainly Epicureans and Stoics whose philosophy was the basis of their morality. Epicureans believed that happiness is the only true aim of human actions. (They appreciated the finer things of life.) The Stoics attempted to remove themselves from the enticements of the world. (They believed that people should do what they think right, regardless of the consequences.)

The cultural climate was tolerant. If something was new, people were interested in it and listened to it.

EMOTIONAL NEEDS

The obvious need is one of growth, but these people were also struggling to understand immortality and life after death. It was not an accident that Paul spoke about the resurrection to these people.

SPIRITUAL BELIEFS

The spiritual world controlled their lives. They saw themselves as pawns of the gods. They believed that harmony of life was maintained when the gods were appeased. When anything went wrong, they tried to discover which god to appease. The altar to the unknown god was used to cover any gods they may have missed.

APPROACHES

Purely emotional appeals or appeals that did not address their beliefs and their ideas would have turned them away.

Their interest would be caught by an approach which represented their culture and their search for new ideas. But it would have to be a clear intellectual presentation.

Paul familiarized himself with the Athenian culture by walking their streets and talking to the people and by drawing on his past training and knowledge. He went to their turf, Mars Hill, to "present" his case before the Council. He indicated respect for their pursuit of knowledge, even drawing on their literature to speak of God's relationship to creation. He spoke of common religious experience.

Then Paul went on to describe God as one who does not need temples or images. He presented a God who had conquered death. He told the people that the day of judgment was at hand and that God who raised Jesus Christ from the dead would judge the world with justice. He called them to repent and make a commitment to God. This meant that they would have to give up their gods and move from following human standards of behavior to following God's standard of righteousness, from salvation through wisdom to salvation through grace.

Paul's presentation was clear. Some believed. One was a member of the Council.

Refer to your biographical study of these people. Do you know people such as these—intellectuals, searchers, people who've "heard it all"? How can you, as an evangelist, translate God's Story of Love to them?

To explore this question, let's try a different setting of the same model. Imagine that Paul is your contemporary. He has just arrived in Washinton, D.C. He has been invited to lecture at a large university. He has come early to spend time on the campus, talking to the students and professors. He goes to the coffee shops and into the bookstores. Everywhere he goes, he discusses ideas, values and religious insights with others. At one end of the campus, he finds a chapel tucked away, empty and unused.

As he visits each department, he discovers many other "altars." Students and professors have made gods out of their academic disciplines. The computer technologists say, "Why pray?—just push a button."

Behavioral scientists say, "We will eventually cure all diseases; we can even create new life!" Paul senses fear, even in their confidence.

He has been scheduled to make a presentation at a faculty meeting prior to his lecture. As Paul speaks there, the professors seem curious and listen attentively. He tells them of an alternative to their trust in technology, an alternative which is personal in a depersonalizing society, an alternative which holds forth life in a world which prophesies self-destruction.

Then Paul invites them to turn from their faith in technology and science to faith in the one true God. The responses are varied. Some call him naive, a crank and a fanatic. Some are interested and ask him to stay after the meeting for a cup of coffee and further discussion. A few are so convinced that what Paul says is true that they are ready to make a commitment. They ask Paul how to find out more about God.

Your areas of witness may not be where Paul's were; but wherever they are, there are people who need to hear God's Story of Love in their own language. And you may be best suited to tell them.

Model No. 2: Peter and the Jews (Acts 3:1-26).

Study the passage, looking for details which describe these people and their cultural identity. Now imagine you are one of these people. Think through the biographical questions at the end of chapter 3. Jot down your responses. Compare them to those which follow. See page 42.

Peter identified himself as one of the crowd, as a Jew. (He claimed descent from Abraham.) He identified Jesus with the God of Abraham and called Jesus the Author of life of whom the prophets had spoken. He went on to say that this same Jesus, the servant of God, had been put to death by God's people.

Peter proposed that they recognize and repent of their participation in the rejection and death of Jesus. They must believe in Jesus as Messiah. Then they would be changed and receive new life.

JEWS AT THE TEMPLE

CULTURAL IDENTITY
These Jews were very religious. They took part in the daily prayers in the temple. They were very conscious of their identity as Jews and faithful in their observation of Jewish law and ritual.

EMOTIONAL NEEDS
They probably had esteem needs, wanting to be reaffirmed as God's chosen people in light of the Christian "heresy."

SPIRITUAL BELIEFS
The traditional Jew believed that God is holy and forgives sin when laws are kept faithfully. Most of the Jews in the crowd Peter addressed probably did not believe Jesus was God's Son.

APPROACHES
Any argument that presented a God different from the God of Israel's patriarchs would not be accepted. Israel's God was to establish a kingdom ruled by a Messiah. A religion without that kind of hope would not be attractive to Jews. But any approach that recognized Jewish beliefs and practices as valid would have hearers.

Refer to your biographical study of these people. Do you know people such as these—people who have rejected Jesus? How can you, as an evangelist, translate God's Story of Love to them?

In this model the Jewish people were in God's house (the temple) but had turned their backs on God's great gift. Peter came onto the scene as an emissary. He spoke of God's love for them, shown through history. To these people, Peter declared the last word of God's love which is always, "Come back!" With this call for repentance is God's commitment to accept and forgive all who do come back (Acts 3:19).

Whenever God works in someone's life, a new version of God's story is written. Yet, all these stories have something in common. They tell of God's saving power and grace.

Notice the differences between the approaches in the two models in this chapter. The differences reflect the language and life experiences of the persons speaking and of those being addressed. But the basic facts remain the same.

The Apostles translated God's Story of Love into the language of their hearers. They invited those who listened to experience God's love—in words they could understand. We must learn to do the same. Like Peter and Paul, we are emissaries seeking to bring reconciliation between people and God. To those who have turned their backs to God's love, often unaware of what they're doing, we share the Good News of God's love when we say, "You are welcome to come back."

"Try Mendelssohn, too," she said. "You'll be haunted forever!"

"How can you do this to me?" he asked, feigning fear.

"Don't blame it on me," she said.

They laughed; the pigeons scattered.

CHAPTER FIVE

"I guess I'm not an atheist, then," he said from under the umbrella.

"I guess not," she said. "Not if you hate God. That's saying there's someone to hate."

They turned the corner and headed toward the restaurant.

"I've never admitted that," he said, "but I know when it started."

She waited at the door of the restaurant as he put the umbrella down.

"It started when my father died of stomach cancer. . . . No one should die like that. Why did God—"

He stopped, unable to finish his question. They went inside, their faces wet.

Barriers can be positive or negative. Some barriers protect us from danger; others block us from what is good and worthwhile. Some people maneuver around barriers. Others cannot. We are now more aware of removing barriers that keep people from living more complete lives. Some people need ramps because stairs are barriers. We should share our faith as a way of removing barriers that keep people from experiencing God's power and presence.

The biblical model in chapter 4 referred to the healing of a begging invalid. His healing led to the arrest of Peter and John and the first conflict between the early Christians and the Jewish leaders. The existence of barriers led to this conflict.

The first barrier was cultural. In those days people regarded miracleworkers as gods because they seemed to have superhuman power. That was why the crowds rushed to Peter and John (Acts 3:11). But this made the trained Jewish leaders jealous of the crude, untutored fisherman. "What power do you have or whose name did you use?" they demanded (Acts 4:7b).

The second barrier was intellectual. This story uses two Greek words for healing. One refers only to physical healing and gives us our word "hygiene" (*hugies*). The other could refer to either physical or spiritual wholeness (*sozo*). It is related to our word, salvation. Peter's accusers wanted to know how the man was healed (*sozo*, Acts 4:9). He replied that the man had been cured (*hugies*, Acts 4:10) in Jesus' name, the same name through which everyone must be saved (*sozo*, Acts 4:12). Peter turned their attention from the physical to the spiritual wholeness God intended in creation. In other words, Jesus is the only one who can make us both physically and spiritually whole.

The third barrier involved their wills. Despite Peter's statement that "Salvation is to be found through him [Jesus Christ] alone" (Acts 4:12a), the leaders of Israel wanted to earn salvation by keeping the law and tradition of their people.

The demands of commitment have been a barrier for many others. The rich young ruler in the model that follows is a case in point. Jesus himself is the "last barrier" we must all encounter. Yet once we put our faith in him, all other barriers crumble.

The Model: Jesus and the rich young ruler (Matthew 19:16-26, Mark 10:17-27, Luke 18:18-27).

Read the text, looking for clues to the cultural environment of the rich young ruler. (If available, refer to a Bible commentary.)

Now think of yourself as the rich young ruler. Refer to the biography at the end of chapter 3 and think through the questions. Jot down your responses. Then compare them to those which follow. See page 47.

Jesus responded to the rich young ruler by reciting the demands of the law. This affirmed the man's "good" life. But Jesus went on to say that something was keeping the man from achieving the perfection he desired. He proposed that the rich young ruler sell all his possessions and distribute the money to the poor. (Jesus was known for this teaching. A good part of the Sermon on the Mount was given to it; see Matthew 6). Jesus asked the young man to turn from his wealth and follow him. Commitment to a good cause is not the same as a commitment to follow Jesus. A commitment to follow someone who did not have "a place to lay his head" required a radical change in life-style.

What Jesus asked the rich young ruler to do was repent. (We have rendered repentance as "radical change" to express the idea in today's language.) Often we think of repentance as merely saying we are sorry for something we were caught doing. This is not what Jesus had in mind. He was not asking people to apologize for a specific act in their lives. He was asking for radical change in their orientation to life. He was saying, "Turn from the security of your own skills, riches and goodness to me."

The ruler's clinging to his world of self and security was his sin. Repentance would mean turning over the part of life he was holding back from God's control. Jesus asked the man to follow him into the kingdom, into a new way of living where priorities were different ("Sell all you have and give the money to the

THE RICH YOUNG RULER

CULTURAL IDENTITY
He was wealthy, well-respected and proper. He may have been a Pharisee, as he was conscious of keeping Jewish law.

EMOTIONAL NEEDS
He recognized a lack in his spiritual life and was eager to grow. In his desire to "do the right thing" he may also have been seeking esteem.

SPIRITUAL BELIEFS
The ruler saw God as the God of the covenant who will fulfill the promises of the kingdom for all who obey the law. In other words, God would bless good people with good things.
He probably did not recognize Jesus as God's Son but as a great teacher.

APPROACHES
The rich young ruler would probably not have listened to anyone who called him a sinner or to anything that would not answer his question. He was a sincere seeker.
His interest could have been caught by an approach which affirmed his status and quest. He would also have responded to a call to high and virtuous standards.

poor") and his life would be radically changed ("then come and follow me," Luke 18:22).

The rich young ruler did not choose to turn from his wealth and sense of righteousness to follow Jesus. The Story of God's Love did not bring the man to faith. But Jesus still responded to the man's questions, answering him in an affirming yet uncompromising way. Jesus' words were not wasted. The man went away—sadly (Luke 18:22). The price was too high. Still, he had heard the message. God was at work in his life.

This model is a good one for the evangelist to keep in mind. You may know people who struggle with faith because of barriers such as the rich young ruler faced. It is helpful to identify these barriers so that we can better share our faith. Think of people you know who may be affected by these barriers:

- Low self-esteem. Some people may not feel "good enough" to become Christian. Because of their life-style, they may feel uncomfortable with church people. There is good news for these people:
  a. Their worth is not measured by their past or by their present but by the fact that God created them as beings of worth.
  b. Jesus cares about them and understands them. The people of Jesus' day did not think he was "good enough." In fact, he was called a sinner because he associated with people who were not accepted by the "good" people of his day.
  c. The church is not made up of people who say they are perfect but of people who have had the courage to say, "I need God and I need the encouragement of other Christians to become who God calls me to be."
- A satisfaction with life as it is. Faith is not important. These people need to see the dramatic effect that faith can have in individual lives.
- Bitterness from past religious experiences.

These are people who have genuinely suffered because of manipulative evangelistic styles, contact with legalistic Christians or incorrect theological training. In such cases, the evangelist would do best to encourage all searchers to tell about these experiences and accept them as part of life. The purpose of this sharing is, as Richard Lischer says, "to help the non-Christian understand that his or her story need not be finished, but that even the story of one who has rejected God can, by the grace of God, begin again."[4]

- Intellectualized religion. Few people are won to faith by argument. A relational, rather than a rational, approach is called for in this situation.

In responding to barriers, it is important to be patient. Barriers to faith are often the result of years of experience. They do not vanish overnight. We must listen and sometimes wait before we invite someone to follow Christ. This can be difficult. As one pastor commented, "My problem is that I plant seeds and then keep digging them up to see how they are doing!" Reactions to pressure to respond can range from annoyance to outright anger. If we are hitting barriers when we present God's Story of Love we may be expecting a decision before the person is ready to make one. This is not to say that every negative response to the Gospel is because of poor timing. There will be times, as in the case of the rich young ruler, when the sincere response is a rejection of God's love offered by Jesus.

Usually people are not open to decision until they feel the need to change. The sensing of the need to change is what is meant by conviction. Conviction is the task of the Holy Spirit. So until there is conviction, our task is to continue to express our witness in word and deed. Until then, resistance should be handled with great understanding and continuing love.

This does not mean we become shy or hesitant

about inviting someone to turn to Christ. Many Christians stop short of giving an invitation because they find it difficult or uncomfortable. You may have established a friendship with another and shared something of your faith; your friend may have even felt convinced of sin and wanted to do something about it. Yet you do not seem able to ask that friend to make the decision that could bring forgiveness and new life. Why?

To give an invitation is to become vulnerable. The person invited may say yes or no. Should the answer be no, the inviter could feel rejected. But think for a moment. An invitation grows out of concern. It opens the door for another to share in something you have. The answer no is not a rejection of you. It is a rejection of what you have offered to share or it may mean that the person is simply not ready to respond. If there is friendship, you can maintain it. And perhaps you can make the offer at another time.

Still we hesitate. We are human. We fear rejection and failure. Realizing this, what can we do about our fears? Here are several things that may help:

1. Be certain you believe God does make a difference in your life and can make a difference in the life of the person to whom you are speaking.
2. Know God's Story of Love and your version of it.
3. Be sensitive to the person to whom you are speaking. Concentrate on his or her needs rather than on yours.
4. Ask God when to join in sharing the story, knowing that the Spirit has already gone ahead to prepare the way.
5. Be willing to risk; if you never risk, you will never grow.

And remember that fears which keep us from what we feel led to do are best overcome not through our strength but through God's strength. As we become partners with the Holy Spirit in expressing the love of God to others, we will be freed of our fears. We will have the love promised in I John 4:18: "Perfect love drives out all fear."

"Why were you crying?" he asked her as they left the restaurant.

"Because you were," she said. "And because I understand your question."

CHAPTER SIX

"You're right. I'm haunted!" he said as he handed her the stack of recordings.

"Which one did you like best?" she asked.

"Christ Lay in Death's Dark Prison."

"Back to Bach."

"Can't beat him," he said, smiling.

"What did you like about it?" she asked.

"Uh—" He hadn't expected her question. Or his answer. "It was real," he said at last.

"Yes," she said, slowly. "It is real."

E arly in this study you identified three persons for whom you would pray and with whom you would seek opportunity to witness. Because they may not yet be Christians, it is helpful to notice Paul's prayer for his own people: "... how I wish with all my heart that my own people might be saved! How I pray to God for them!" (Romans 10:1). Though the Jews had rejected Jesus, Paul was convinced that God had not rejected them. Therefore, sharing God's concern, Paul desired and prayed for their salvation.

But Paul did more than pray for them. He told them how not to be, as well as how to be, saved.

He told them they could not be saved by
- good deeds (Romans 10:2-4) or
- well-developed theology (Romans 10:5-7).

They could be saved by
- the work of the "The Word" (Spirit) in them (Romans 10:8) and
- the response of confession and belief (Romans 10:9-10).

In one short verse Paul said all that is necessary for someone to become a child of God:

"If you confess that Jesus is Lord and believe that God raised him from death, you will be saved" (Romans 10:9).

To "confess that Jesus is Lord" is to put your life under his control. To "believe that God raised him" is to believe that God whose power gave new life to Jesus can give the believer new life as well. While this sounds simple, we know that we cannot come to faith on our own. Therefore, God gives us the Holy Spirit through whose work we are convicted.

Generally, people will not commit themselves to anything unless they are persuaded of its validity. When people feel persuaded they are under conviction. Too often we think of conviction as involving guilt and judgment. Conviction may mean that. But it can also mean being persuaded. Conviction drives people to seek some way to act on what they are convinced about. Consequently, conviction brings a person to a point of decision.

It is not the job of the evangelist to convince someone of his or her need to change. God has put within all of us a standard of what is right and a sense of accountability for our actions. Paul calls this our conscience (Romans 2:14-15). Conscience may be dulled by environment but it can be activated again by the Spirit. Ultimately, only the Holy Spirit can sensitize a conscience and convict someone of the need for salvation. But the Spirit may use evangelists in the process.

In what ways does the Spirit work through us to make someone aware of his or her need for Christ?

- Through a deep friendship. Christian friendship demonstrates unconditional love. This love could make someone wonder why this friend is so different. It might lead someone to ask, "Why do you care? Why don't you give up on me? You always seem available. You always seem to understand."

- Through something read, heard or seen. Many times in dealing with people who enjoy books, music, art or theater, we can suggest something to read, hear or see that would be of help in a particular circumstance. We may suggest a certain Bible passage. Or we may be able to make a statement or ask a question that leads to discussion.

- Through acts of caring. Our deeds can become keys that open doors that have been locked: a meal for someone not feeling well, a visit to someone lonely. People are hungry, unemployed and hurting. As Christians we need to care about people facing these situations. The only way people will believe God can be with them is if we are with them. James emphasized this by saying that if we seek to minister to spiritual needs to the neglect of physical needs, it will profit us nothing (James 2:14-17).

When people become convinced (convicted) of their need for Christ, our role is to be there to share God's story with them in language that will be understood. Paul reminds us of the joy of this responsiblity in his exclamation, "How wonderful is the coming of messengers who bring good news!" (Romans 10:15b).

Sharing the Good News of God's love at the point of conviction is like serving the last course of a progressive dinner. The Spirit has created the hunger. We simply serve the meal.

Knowing this gives confidence. We are responsible for contacts, not conviction. And even our contacts are made in response to the leading of the Holy Spirit. The Spirit does not abandon us to people with whom we have nothing in common or to those who will be hostile to us. (Hostile reaction comes when we are insensitive to either the Spirit or the friend with whom we share.)

Up to this point we have assumed that the evangelist is very well-acquainted with those to whom he or she witnesses and that the evangelist seeks to share God's story based on what he or she knows of the listener.

There are occasions, however, when we will share God's story with people we do not know well. We will sometimes be led to people impromptu. But our training can still serve us. We need to listen, determine needs and respond in language which can be understood.

In the model which follows, you will read about Philip initiating a contact with a stranger from a different culture. But as you study you will discover that Philip and the Ethiopian were brought together by the Spirit of God.

The Model: Philip and the Ethiopian official (Acts 8:26-39).

Note: The church has been unwilling and unable to witness to public officials. It is interesting to see the many evangelistic encounters in Acts between Christians and public officials. (This may help you think of similar people in your own community to whom you can witness.)

Think of yourself as the Ethiopian. Refer to the biography at the end of chapter 3 and consider the questions. Jot down your answers and compare them to the information which follows. See page 56.

THE ETHIOPIAN OFFICIAL

CULTURAL IDENTITY

He was a convert to Judaism, a religious man searching for answers. He had been on a pilgrimage to Jerusalem. He was open to new ideas.

Ethiopia was an ancient kingdom located in the Sudan (Africa). Its inhabitants were of African descent and were called Nubians. Officials who served queens were often eunuchs. This eunuch was the treasurer for Candace, the queen.

EMOTIONAL NEEDS

It appears that the official had a need to grow, to be challenged.

SPIRITUAL BELIEFS

He saw God as being satisfied with worship. But he also wondered if there was more to God than that.

APPROACHES

The official had a need to know. He would have rejected any approach that ignored his questions. He would have responded to an approach that would make the pieces of the puzzle come together and give faith a personal dimension.

Philip answered the Ethiopian's questions. He put the man's experience in God's context and introduced him to Jesus. He proposed that the official, as a symbol of his commitment, be baptized.

There are three key lessons for us in this model:

One: Philip, in response to the Spirit, made initial contact with the official.

Two: Philip began where the man was—in Isaiah. (And although we may not encounter people sitting around reading Isaiah, we are challenged to meet people where they are, to answer the questions they have at that moment and to believe that the Holy Spirit leads us each step of the way.)

Three: It is easy to think that repentance only means turning away from something bad. However, good people who focus on good things (but not on Christ) must also repent. They must change their focus. The official was looking for the Messiah in the history of Israel and in the ritual of the temple. Philip told him that Jesus was the fulfillment of history and the way to God. The official, convicted by the Holy Spirit working through Philip, changed his focus. For him, that was repentance, acceptance and thus salvation.

The story of Philip and the Ethiopian is a beautiful story of faith. In response to conviction, there was conversion. Would that all evangelism led to such a result!

But it does not. There was, remember, the story of the rich young ruler who was convicted and did not repent. This will happen. It sometimes has nothing to do with the evangelist. (Christ was the evangelist in that case!) Even so, we must not forget those who do not respond to God's story. There is no reason we cannot continue the friendship and pray that the barriers to faith will someday be overcome.

"That's beautiful," he said, as she finished her story. "I wish I could believe as you do."

"You can," she said.

"How?" he asked. "How do you believe?"

"You have to take a chance. You have to be vulnerable. And let God back into your life."

CHAPTER SEVEN

"Okay," he said. "All right. I can believe that God is my creator. And I can believe that God loves me . . . . But why didn't God love my father?"

She sat in silence.

"Look how he suffered. Look how he died," he said, demanding her to answer.

Her answer was a whisper. "You don't think God loved Jesus?"

"Oh," he said, seeing the pain on her face.

Her question was his answer.

Earlier in this book you had the opportunity to think through your own conversion and faith experience. For some Christians, especially for those who have grown up in the church, it is difficult to pinpoint a conversion experience because of the way it has often been described. We must remember that conversion describes a change.

Apartments are converted to condominiums and vans to campers; fuels are converted into energy and raw materials into products. We talk about converting software and grid-point data. Used in this sense, conversion means something is changed from one form, shape or purpose into another. But what do we mean when we talk about a person being converted?

The word "conversion" is not used very often in the

Bible. But the idea is found on almost every page. Conversion is the idea of changing. And the Bible is a book about change.

Jesus used the example of children when talking about conversion. He told his disciples they must change and become childlike, trusting him as a child does (Matthew 18:4-5). Whoever does that, he said, will be converted.

Christian conversion, then, means to come to a point of trusting Jesus Christ as the Master of our lives rather than trusting ourselves. It is sensing that we need to belong to God through Jesus (conviction). And it is turning from one source of authority to another (repentance). When we do this, we are forgiven. We are converted. This definition allows for those who have grown into faith, for those who point to a number of events as life-changing and for those who have experienced a very sudden and radical change.

It would be simpler for us as evangelists if everyone were converted in the same way. But the Gospel meets people where they are. And people experience conversion in different ways depending on the environment in which they function, their emotional needs, their spiritual background and the working of the Holy Spirit in their lives. Therefore, we need to be able to help those whose experience is different from ours. Paul realized this and was thus able to relate God's story to different people in different ways. He never expected anyone else to have a "Damascus Road" conversion experience (Acts 9:1-19). That is because Paul understood conversion.

On his way to Damascus to arrest the Jewish heretics who had become Christians, something very unusual happened to Paul. A flash of light brighter than the sun blinded him and struck him down. Lying on the road, Paul heard a voice, the voice of Jesus.

For Paul, the combination of light and voice had great significance. As a Jew, he knew it was God who spoke to Moses out of a burning bush (Exodus 3:2). It was God who spoke on the mountain in the midst of lightning and thunder and gave the law to Israel (Exodus 19). And it was God who spoke to the boy Samuel before the light of the lampstand went out (I Samuel 3).

The result? Paul's encounter with Jesus, presented in an image familiar in Judaism, changed his life. He described this change very graphically in his testimony to Agrippa (Acts 26:18). As Paul had been changed, so he now called on others to change, "to turn from darkness to the light."

The Bible speaks of the turning as believing and repentance. To repent is to turn away from something. To believe is to turn to something or someone. These two acts add up to our part in the conversion equation. God's part is conviction, forgiveness and empowerment by the Holy Spirit.

God does not have a list of certain sins of which we must repent in order to be saved. God calls us to turn from whatever it is that keeps us from living under the authority of Christ. For some of us this requires a major change and for some only a small change. What we turn from depends on how we have lived as we walked from God into the shadows of darkness. Regardless of how radical or slight that first turn is, "It is by God's grace that you have been saved through faith. It is not the result of your own efforts, but God's gift, so that no one can boast about it" (Ephesians 2:8-9).

Because of the grace of God, because of how God comes to individuals, experiences will be different. That is what this book is about. It is about a story with meaning for everyone.

The following models illustrate this. The evangelist is the same in each case (Paul). But God's Story is translated, in each case, to the individual.

The Models: Paul and Lydia, Paul and the slave girl, Paul and the Philippian jailer (Acts 16:11-40).

Choose one of the three model subjects to study, preferably one whose conversion experience is different from your own. Lydia (like the Ethiopian) "grew" into faith by taking a final step; the slave girl was saved from a desperate situation in which she had been used and abused by society (as was the paralytic who begged at the temple gate); the jailer came to faith because of a single life-changing experience in which he recognized the Spirit of God (as did the Samaritan woman).

Read the passage, looking for details that describe the person you've chosen to study. Refer to a Bible commentary for more information.

Think of yourself as this person, using the biography at the end of chapter 3 as a guide. Then refer to the following responses (appropriate to the model you studied). See pages 63, 64 and 65.

Note that response marked conversion. The climax of these faith stories and of any faith story is clearly the decision to transfer loyalties, to reverse directions, to commit to a new path.

This change brings about transformation in personal loyalties, priorities and relationships. Christians see others in terms of who they can become by the working of the Holy Spirit in their lives to convict, convert and empower them as children of God.

Our task as evangelists is to see people in this way—to love them and to be the bearer of God's love to them. We are to "be with them," representing Jesus in the flesh as Jesus represented God in the flesh.

Our preparation for this task consists partly of living in the world and identifying with individuals in the world. It means listening to others, identifying their backgrounds, needs and beliefs and, as a result, being able to personalize God's Story of Love to them.

Throughout history this kind of evangelism has been modeled. By Paul, Peter, Augustine, Luther, Joanna

LYDIA

CULTURAL IDENTITY
Lydia was a businesswoman, a family person and a generous host. She had a Greek name but was worshiping with Jews. She was probably part of the group of non-Jews (referred to elsewhere in Acts such as the Ethiopian official) who were drawn to Judaism by its high morality and view of God.

EMOTIONAL NEEDS
She had a need to grow which was evident in her spiritual searching.

SPIRITUAL BELIEFS
Lydia believed God to be wonderful, loving and gracious, a faithful God who answered prayer.
But God belonged to the Jews.

APPROACHES
Approaches that made little of God or belittled her own belief would have turned Lydia away. An approach that made God personal would have great appeal for her as well as any approach that admitted her into Judaism.

●

Paul's approach to Lydia was to join her in prayer to the God in whom they both believed. In so doing, he reinforced the belief she already had. Then he told her the Story of God's Love for her displayed in Jesus, the Messiah of both Jew and Gentile. He encouraged her to believe in Jesus and to announce her intention to follow him by being baptized.

THE SLAVE GIRL

CULTURAL IDENTITY
This girl was a victim, exploited by a superstitious society and by greedy men. Her identity and self-worth were those of a slave; she had little control over her own life.

EMOTIONAL NEEDS
She needed affection. Her needs for affection were not being met by her owners. Yet she was dependent on them and therefore trapped, fearful of losing her security.

SPIRITUAL BELIEFS
God was unknown except through the words that came unbidden from her mouth.

APPROACHES
The girl would have been turned away had she heard that God caused her to be the way she was, out of control, possessed. She would be interested to hear of a God who loved her and could set her free.

●

Paul shocked her out of her fear. And in the name of Christ he set her free. This meant she had to let go of those who held her captive, both within and without. She had to face a loss of physical security.

In order to be truly changed, the girl would have had to acknowledge her Savior. The account does not specifically say that this is what happened. It is reasonable to assume that Paul did not leave her "empty," considering the consequences suggested in Luke 11:24-26.

THE PHILIPPIAN JAILER

CULTURAL IDENTITY
The jailer was a Roman civil employee. He may have been a soldier. As a jailer he was probably not easily moved by people's problems or by pain and suffering. He had a job to do and was aware of the penalty for not doing it (execution). He found identity in his job and was probably a respected citizen.

EMOTIONAL NEEDS
At the time of this account his greatest need was for security—to save his physical life, put in jeopardy by the supposed escape of his prisoners.

SPIRITUAL BELIEFS
As a Roman this jailer probably believed in many gods and in their supernatural powers. He may have construed the earthquake to be an action of angry gods.

APPROACHES
The jailer would have been turned away by any approach that would scare him even more or make him think he was to blame for what had happened. He would have responded to a God who was fair and would treat him fairly, a God who could save his life.

●

Paul offered the jailer salvation, both physical and spiritual. He gave him an explanation of the supernatural which was given credence by the very presence of Paul and Silas. (They had not run away.)

The jailer believed and was baptized.

Moore, Walter Rauschenbusch, D. T. Niles. Similarly, it is modeled today by Sunday church school teachers, youth workers, parents, co-workers, friends and pastors. Concern for others, lived and stated, brings others to respond to an invitation to faith.

For evangelism is more than a program, it is *being there*, and because of that, *being heard*. It is listening and in the listening, finding the means to translate the message.

At the beginning of this book you were asked to pray and work toward helping three friends come to faith in Jesus Christ. Whatever their responses have been, your concern for them (and for others!) does not end with this book. Evaluate what has happened as you've shared. Don't abandon them, no matter what their response has been. Think of three other people you know who need to hear the *Good* News of God's Story of Love. And continue to pray for the leading of the Holy Spirit in your efforts and in the lives of all of those with whom you may share.

Evangelism at its best represents the essence of Christian faith, mission and experience. It tells the story of a God who loves us and offers us life instead of death. It represents, for those who communicate that story, a divine mission. And it represents a process that brings people to faith in Jesus Christ and to the integration of that faith with life. It is a high calling with high stakes. Yet we need not be nervous about our witness. God has the highest stake in our efforts. And God will not forsake us. Jesus said: "Do not be anxious how you are to speak or what you are to say; for what you are to say will be given to you in that hour; for it is not you who speak, but the Spirit of your Father speaking through you" (Matthew 19:19, 20 RSV).

Taking hold of that promise, we can evangelize as we are led by the Spirit of a God who wills "that every human being should find salvation and come to know the truth."[5]

Now it was his turn to be silent.

"God doesn't promise us lives free from pain," she said.

"I know," he said. "I'm sorry."

"God forgives."

"Then maybe God will forgive me," he said. "I want . . . to believe."

She hugged him then, thanking God for new life.

And the music of faith resounded in the park.

GUIDE FOR GROUPS

"Everyday evangelists" can often become more effective if they have the encouragement and prayers of other evangelists. This support may be gained from an informal group of like-minded friends or from a group which meets for the specific purpose of study. The following guide has been designed for use with this book by such a group for a six-week study.

If the group is meeting together for the first time, participants should meet briefly to discuss the group's purpose, schedule and leadership style. (Each session should have a group leader but leadership can pass from person to person if needed.) Decide who will publicize the meetings.

The preliminary meeting should also include discussion of the group's future. Relationships of trust are more likely to occur if the group will continue to meet regularly for sharing and prayer after the study of the book is completed. Decide whether or not to plan a refreshment time after the meetings. Designate the responsibility for refreshments.

The leader of the first study should remind group members to read the introduction and chapter 1 before the first study and to bring their copies of the book with them.

INTRODUCTION AND CHAPTER 1

To the Leader

If your group has not met prior to this study, you will want to set aside time for handling organizational details. All group members should have read the introduction and first chapter before beginning the study below. Make sure there will be at least one modern translation of the Bible and a chalkboard (or a pad of newsprint) available.

Discussion Starters

• As the group arrives, ask individuals to find a partner (or two) and get better acquainted by discussing why, when and how they joined their church. Write the question ("Why, when and how did you join the church?") on a chalkboard or piece of newsprint.

• When all persons are present and each has had at least a few minutes to respond to the questions above, direct the small group to read the illustration from the introduction (page 7) and share their past experience with or feelings about evangelism. Ask: "Were there some approaches that made you comfortable; some that made you feel uncomfortable?" (Allow 10-15 minutes for this activity.)

• Call the group together. Summarize how group members feel about evangelism by listing reactions on the chalkboard or on a piece of newsprint.

Study

• Define what is meant by evangelism for the purpose of this study. (It is the one-to-one sharing of God's Good News that makes faith an option for those with whom faith is shared.) Write your definition on the chalkboard or newsprint.

• This book offers "The Story of Love" as a way that evangelism can be done. Have group members turn to "The Story of Love" on page 14. Assign one person to read the left-hand column and one to read the right-hand column, responsively (for example, *Love Expressed* followed by *Love Rejected*).

• Tell the group members that you are going to have them repeat "The Story of Love" to each other in their own words. Give them a moment to review the story individually. Then have them return to their small groups and begin their Storytelling. (Allow 10 minutes for this activity. But make sure each person has had an opportunity to tell the story before time is called.)

• Call the group together. Encourage group members to share their feelings about telling "The Story of Love." Was it difficult? Why or why not?

• Remind group members that "The Story of Love" is never told in a vacuum. Have someone read John 14:16-29 in a modern translation of the Bible.

Prayer

Where there is no sincere prayer, there will be ineffective evangelism. Spend time praying together for the work you have begun in this study.

CHAPTER 2

To the Leader

Check with your group ahead of time and determine whether they want to do the faith autobiographies and stories prior to your meeting time or during it. Adjust the following plans accordingly.

Provide blank paper for each person. Try to secure several tape recorders.

Discussion Starters

• Spend some time sharing what group members discovered in completing their autobiographies and "Steps of Faith" or "Faith Stories." (Or use your meeting time to complete these exercises. Directions are given in chapter 2.) Ask: "What single event or person in your life was the most influential in your coming to faith?

Why?" Encourage each group member to share.

Study

• Distribute paper to each person. Direct the group to outline "The Story of Love," listing the categories in both columns as shown on page 14. Instruct them to leave the left-hand column (GOD'S INITIATIVE) blank. In the right-hand column (HUMAN RESPONSE), have each person list specific life experiences in the appropriate categories (*Love Rejected, Love Accepted, Love Obeyed*). Autobiographies, "Steps of Faith" and "Faith Stories" can be used as reference data in this exercise.

• Now divide the group into pairs (or groups of three). Have each person share his or her HUMAN RESPONSE in "The Story of Love." Remind them to avoid using religious phrases ("accepted Christ", "saved", etc.). Group members should give feedback to each other regarding the clarity, timeliness and interest-level of their stories. If tape recorders are available, each person can join in the critique of his or her own story-telling. (Allow at least 15 minutes for this activity.)

• Have the small groups share their experiences with the whole group. Ask: "How did this experience affect you? How did it seem to affect others in your small group?"

Prayer

Share prayer concerns. In chapter 2, readers were asked to think of three people with whom they can share their faith. Spend time praying for these individuals and for each other.

CHAPTER 3

To the Leader

Since much of this meeting is designed as a Bible study, ask group members to bring Bibles. (Bring several for those who forget. Modern translations are preferable.) Refer to a Bible commentary[6] as you study John 4 in preparation for the meeting. Record historical and cultural background as well as any information about the Samaritan woman.

You will need a chalkboard or large pad of newsprint and blank paper.

Discussion Starters

• Call attention to the "park bench" storyline that runs throughout the book. What is happening in this encounter? As a group, react to the story·thus far.

• Encourage group members to share any "park bench" encounters they've had with people of other faiths. What was their reaction to the experience? Why?

Study

• Have each person read John 4:1-42 silently.

• Go over the information about the setting of this passage provided on page 26. Give the group further background from the resources you have studied.

• Now turn to the biography form at the end of chapter 3 and discuss it. Imagine that the Samaritan woman is your contemporary. Have someone list the responses on a chalkboard or newsprint pad. Relax and enjoy doing this exercise together.

• Review the approach that Jesus used to tell God's Story to the Samaritan woman. Why was it successful?

• Instruct group members to spend time now to look at (or fill out if desired) the biography form for at least one of the three persons with whom they have decided to share faith. Provide paper as necessary.

Prayer

Divide the group into smaller groups for sharing and prayer. Use the completed biographies to pray in a specific way for each other and those who are experiencing your friendship.

CHAPTER 4

To the Leader

Contact two members of the group in advance to request their participation in the role-playing exercise explained below. Give them an idea of the parts they will be playing and their opening lines so they can "create their characters."

Be sure to have blank paper and a newsprint pad or chalkboard available for use.

Discussion Starters

• Begin the meeting by doing word-association. Tell the group to give spontaneous one-word responses to the following words (list them one at a time on the chalkboard or newsprint pad): strike, record, run, church, God, sin. Jot down the responses opposite the words.

• Say: "The word-association exercise points out that words do not mean the same thing to everyone. This is especially true of religious (or theological) words."

Now divide the group into pairs. Provide blank paper. List the following words on the chalkboard or newsprint pad: conviction, repentance, conversion, reconciliation. Have pairs brainstorm definitions for these words. Then reconvene the group and have the pairs share their definitions. See how they compare to these definitions: Conviction—"to be persuaded about." Repentance—"to turn away from." Conversion—"to turn to; to become. "Reconciliation—"to reorder relationship."

Make the point that being able to define these religious words is essential if they are to be used and understood.

Study

• Have your two role-players sit up in the front or center of your group. One is to play the part of an unchurched teenager who is preoccupied with the problem of what to do after high school graduation. The other (the evangelist) is an adult neighbor of casual acquaintance who knows the teenager will soon graduate.

The task of the evangelist is to share some part of God's Story of Love with the teenager. Cue the evangelist to say: "So, what are your plans after graduation?" The teenager replies, miserably, "Why does everyone ask me that?" Allow the role-play to go on for three to four minutes or until the players exhaust their roles.

• Discuss what happened. Ask: "What needs were evident? How were these needs addressed? Could they have been addressed another way? What did the evangelist say that seemed to cause the greatest understanding? What else could have been said? How was the 'translation'?" As the leader, be sure to affirm the role-players and thank them for their help.

• Have the group get back into pairs. Give them the following situation to role-play: One is a young adult, struggling with financial problems, who says: "Life is too complicated. I just can't handle it anymore." The other (the evangelist) is a co-worker. (Allow three to five minutes.)

• Call the group back together and debrief. How did the participants feel—as evangelists? as persons being evangelized?

• Ask: "How has this experience affected your feelings about doing evangelism?"

Prayer

Direct the group to pray responsively, in short phrases or sentences, praising God and asking for guidance in translating the Story to others. Close the prayer time by reading Matthew 10:19, 20 and adding, "Amen."

CHAPTER 5

To the Leader

Arrive at the meeting place far enough ahead of time to prepare for the "discussion starter" described below. You may want to ask someone to help you "set up."

Be sure there are several modern translations of the Bible available as well as a chalkboard or newsprint pad and blank paper.

Discussion Starters

• Put up some kind of physical barrier in the meeting room so that it is difficult for persons to enter the room. (Use chairs, toys, room dividers, etc.) You may even want to post a sign reading, "Enter at Your Own Risk." Note how those who enter respond to the barriers. (Enlist the first person who arrives to help you in this observation.) When everyone is present, share your observations with the group.

• Ask: "What are the barriers to faith? What are some barriers you faced before you believed? Have you encountered any barriers in the three people with whom you have shared the Gospel?"

Study

• Ask how the group feels about the continuing "park bench" storyline in the book. Then ask: "What barriers to faith are present in this story? How are they being handled?"

• Divide the group into groups of four (depending on the size of your group). Provide each group with a piece of blank paper. Ask them to read Ephesians 2:1-10.

• While they are reading, write on the chalkboard or newsprint pad: "I live a good life. I help people. Isn't that what a Christian is?" Have the groups work together to decide (and record) what barriers to faith exist in that statement. Then have them decide (and jot down) how they could invite that person to turn to Christ. (Allow 10-15 minutes.)

• Reconvene the large group. Have a representative from each group report their findings and transfer their responses to the chalkboard or newsprint. Ask: "How do you feel about actually inviting someone to turn to Christ? Why? How can these feelings help you in giving that invitation?"

Prayer

Have group members share prayer requests about their work as evangelists. Direct the group to respond to each request by repeating together, "Perfect love drives out all fear."

Close the meeting with a single prayer.

CHAPTERS 6 AND 7

To the Leader

In this meeting, you will conclude the study of this book. If you have not included a refreshment time in your other meetings, you may want to plan one for the close of this meeting.

Be sure blank paper is on hand. Also, gather some hymnbooks ahead of time. Choose a hymn of dedication to sing at the end of the meeting.

Discussion Starters

• Share reactions to the "park bench" storyline. Evaluate the evangelism done in that story. Ask: "What did the man need? How did the Holy Spirit work in the man's life to make him aware (convict him) of this need? How did the woman (the evangelist) respond?"

• Have group members evaluate their own experiences of sharing faith (since the beginning of this study) with one or two other members of the group. Suggest that they answer some of these questions: "Was it easier or more difficult than you thought it would be to share? Why? Were there any surprises in your experiences? How did you handle them? In what ways will your experiences affect your future evangelistic efforts?"

Study

• Gather back together. Point out that faith is sometimes shared "on-the-spot," as seen in the models in chapters 6 and 7. Ask: "How do you feel about doing that kind of evangelism? What principles of sharing faith would be useful in an on-the-spot situation?" (If the group does not suggest anything, offer the following principles: the ability to listen, translate language, discern needs, show concern, sense barriers, etc.)

• Now ask each group member to tell with whom they would be more comfortable in sharing on-the-spot—someone such as Lydia or the Ethiopian, (religious people)? the slave girl (the desperate person)? or the jailer (the seeker who has questions)? Ask them to form small groups based on their choices. Then assign the groups a "type" other than that with which they are comfortable. (For example, if persons are most comfortable with the Lydia "type," assign them the slave girl or the jailer "type"). Explain that this is a learning exercise and is not meant to be threatening.

• Direct the groups to read the scriptural text and study the cultural/emotional/spiritual characteristics of their "type" in chapters 6 and 7 (pages 55-56 and 61-65). As they finish the study, go to each group, distribute blank paper and instruct each person to think of an individual he or she knows who is similar to the person in the model. Refer them to the biography at the end of chapter 3 and have them respond to the questions with that person in mind. (Allow 15-20 minutes for this exercise.)

• Call the group back together. Ask for several persons to share what they would do if given the opportunity to share with the person they chose in the exercise above.

Prayer

Call the group together. Encourage group members to share prayer requests concerning the above exercise in addition to other requests.

Close the meeting by singing a hymn of dedication.

FOOTNOTES

[1]George Peck, "A Theological Environment for Effective Evangelism," lectures presented to the American Baptist Evangelism Team, Clearwater, Florida, January, 1983.

[2]Ibid.

[3]David W. Ausburger, *Communicating Good News* (Scottdale, Pa: Herald Press, 1972), p. 33.

[4]Richard Lischer, *Speaking of Jesus* (Philadelphia: Fortress Press, 1982), p. 71.

[5]George Peck, "A Theological Environment for Effective Evangelism," lectures presented to the American Baptist Evangelism Team, Clearwater, Florida, January, 1983.

[6]These may be found in your church, school or public library: *The New Bible Commentary: Revised* (Wm. B. Eerdmans Publishing Co., Grand Rapids, MI); *The Abingdon Bible Commentary* (Abingdon Press, Nashville, TN); *The Layman's Bible Commentary* (John Knox Press, Atlanta, GA).